Published By Robert Corbin

@ Larry Lewis

Pizza: Best Pizza Churned Out of Your Kitche

All Right RESERVED

ISBN 978-87-94477-80-2

TABLE OF CONTENTS

Antipasto Pizza 1

Apple And Bacon Pita Pizzas... 2

Whole Wheat Pizza With Chicken And Scallions 4

Garlic Mushrooms And Basil Pizza 6

Roasted Vegetables Pizza 8

Pasta With Mediterranean Meatballs 9

Thai Beef Shirataki Stir-Fry 14

Cauliflower Crust Pizza 17

Spelt Pizza Bianco With Jersey Royals 21

The Super Gluten Free Pizza Crust + Sauce 25

Gluten Free Pizza Power... 28

Kale-Artichoke Pizza 34

Sausage-Pepper Pizza Coconut Tuna Zucchini Bake....... 37

Creamy Garlic Shrimp With Angel Hair 38

Parsnip Soup 42

Spinach Soup 44

Almond Skillet Bread 46

Just-Like-Regular Keto Bread 48

Peanut Flour Bread 50

Apple Goat Cheese And Pecan Pizza 52

Apple Walnut Pizza With Caramelized Onions 53

Artichoke Pizzas With Lemony Green Bean Salad 56

Beefed Up Pizza Wedges With Pepperoni And Black Olives 58

Beef Paleo Pizza With Portobello Mushrooms 60

Wild Rockets, Bacon And Mushroom Paleo Pizza 62

Beef Ragu With Veggie Pasta 64

Classic Beef Lasagna 66

Creamy Sun-Dried & Parsnip Noodles 69

No Yeast Pizza Dough 70

Rainbow Pizzas 72

Pumpkin Pizza With Zucchini And Nuts 74

Gluten-Free Pizza With Fresh Mozzarella, Olives, Basil, And Anaheim Peppers 77

Gluten-Free Tuscan-Style Pizza 81

Pepperoni Pizza 85

Vegan Marguerite Pizza With Gluten-Free Crust 89

Creamy Salmon Shirataki Fettucine 95

Creamy Mussel With Shirataki 98

Roasted Jalapeno Soup 101

Cucumber Soup 103

Sweetcorn Soup 105

Baking Powder Bread 107

Cloud Flatbread 109

Lemon Bread With Blueberries 111

Artichoke Spinach Pizza 113

Arugula Pesto Ricotta And Smoked Mozzarella Pizza .. 115

Bacon And Egg Breakfast Pizza 117

Pitta Pizzas 119

Pork, Gorgonzola & Garlic Butter Pizza 120

Gluten-Free Cauliflower Crust Pesto Pizza 123

Pepperoni Pizza Gluten Free, Dairy Free And Egg Free 126

Gluten Free Pizza Crackers 129

Spaghetti Squash Pizza Crust 132

Gluten Free Pizza With A Rice Base 135

Oat Gluten-Free Pizza Crust 138

Beef Alfredo Squash Spaghetti 141

Beef-Asparagus Shirataki Mix 144

Garlic-Butter Steak Bites 147

Green Pesto Pasta 149

Chicken And Broccoli 150

Chicken And Rice 152

Antipasto Pizza

Ingredients:

- 2 cup diced salami or deli ham
- 4 cup sliced banana peppers
- 4 cup sliced black olives
- 4 cup sun-dried tomatoes in oil, drained and chopped
- (12-inch) prebaked pizza crust
- 4 cup refrigerated pesto
- 4 cup chopped artichoke hearts
- 1/2 cups shredded Mozzarella cheese

Directions:
1. Spread pizza crust evenly with 1/4 cup pesto. Sprinkle evenly with remaining Ingredients:.
2. Bake at 450° for 12 to 14 minutes or until cheese is melted.

Apple And Bacon Pita Pizzas

Ingredients:

- cups thinly sliced fuji apple
- tablespoons grated fresh parmesan cheese
- tablespoons chopped walnuts, toasted
- teaspoon chopped fresh thyme
- (6-inch) whole-wheat pitas
- teaspoons olive oil
- ounces cheddar cheese, shredded (about 1/cup)
- applewood-smoked bacon slices, chopped and cooked

Directions:

1. Preheat broiler to high.
2. Broil pitas 1 minute or until lightly golden. Remove from oven; carefully flip pitas over.

Brush evenly with olive oil. Sprinkle cheddar over pitas; arrange apple slices over cheese.

3. Sprinkle Parmesan cheese, walnuts, thyme, and bacon evenly over apples. Return to oven; broil 1 to 2 minutes.

Whole Wheat Pizza With Chicken And Scallions

Ingredients:

- Chicken breast
- 1 ball entire wheat pizza batter
- 3 new Scallions
- 1/2 cup farm dressing
- 1/2 cup Buffalo Chicken sauce
- 1 tbsp butter

Directions:

1. Preheat your broiler to 425 degrees F.
2. In a little pan, add the spread, chicken and bison chicken sauce and cook for 7 minutes.
3. Grease a treat sheet with olive oil and spot the mixture on top to work and move it out.
4. Pour the farm dressing over the batter and top it with scallions.

5. Add the sauce and cooked chicken on the pizza dough.
6. Use up the excess scallions to cover the dough.
7. Pour extra chicken sauce on the pizza and heat in the stove for around 20 minutes.
8. Slice the Whole Wheat Pizza with Chicken and Scallions into quarters and serve while hot.

Garlic Mushrooms And Basil Pizza

Ingredients:

- 1 egg
- 1 teaspoon basil
- ½ head cauliflower
- 1 clove garlic
- 1 teaspoon oregano

Directions:
1. Preheat your broiler to 400 degrees F.
2. Grease a treat sheet with olive oil.
3. Chop the cauliflower florets into lumps and add them to a food processor.
4. Pulse the food processor to change over the florets into rice like consistency.
5. In a skillet, sauté the cauliflower until it turns translucent.

6. In a medium-sized bowl, consolidate the leftover fixings in addition to the cooked cauliflower.
7. Prepare the mixture and heat in the broiler for around 30 minutes.
8. Remove the outside and top it with mushrooms and basil.
9. Broil the cooked pizza for around 5 minutes to relax the mushrooms.
10. Cut the pizza into sensible cuts and serve while hot.

Roasted Vegetables Pizza

Ingredients:

- 1 tablespoon rosemary leaves Pepper
- 6 cups Roasted vegetables of decision
- Almond Flour
- 1 pound pizza mixture (locally acquired)
- Olive oil Salt

Directions:

1. Preheat your stove to 475 degrees F.
2. On a material paper, roll the mixture and spot different vegetables on top.
3. Drizzle some olive oil and add the rosemary leaves.
4. Bake the batter in the stove for around 25 minutes and serve on a plate while hot.

Pasta With Mediterranean Meatballs

Ingredients:

- 6 garlic cloves, minced
- Salt and black pepper to taste
- ½ tsp coriander powder
- ¼ tsp nutmeg powder
- 1 tbsp smoked paprika
- 1 ½ tsp fresh ginger paste
- 1 tsp cumin powder
- ½ tsp cayenne pepper
- 1 ½ tsp turmeric powder
- ½ tsp cloves powder
- 4 tbsp chopped cilantro
- 4 tbsp chopped scallion s

- 4 tbsp chopped parsley
- ¼ cup almond flour
- ¼ cup olive oil
- 1 cup shredded mozzarella cheese
- 1 egg yolk
- 3 tbsp olive oil
- 2 yellow onions, chopped
- 6 garlic cloves, minced
- 2 tbsp unsweetened tomato paste
- 2 large tomatoes, chopped
- ¼ tsp saffron powder
- 2 cinnamon sticks
- 4 ½ cups chicken broth
- Salt and black pepper to taste

- 2 cups pork rinds
- 1 lb ground beef
- 1 egg
- ¼ cup almond milk
- 1 cup crumbled feta cheese for serving

Directions:

1. Pour the cheese into a medium safe-microwave bowl and melt in the microwave for 2 minutes while stirring at 20-second intervals until fully melted.
2. Remove the bowl and allow cooling for 1 minute only to warm the cheese but not cool completely. Mix in the egg yolk until well combined.
3. Lay parchment paper on a flat surface, pour the cheese mixture on top and cover with another parchment paper. Using a rolling pin, flatten the dough into 1/8-inch thickness.

4. Take off the parchment paper and cut the dough into spaghetti strands. Place in a bowl and refrigerate overnight.
5. When ready to cook, bring 2 cups of water to a boil in a medium saucepan and add the pasta. Cook for 40 seconds to 1 minute and then drain through a colander.
6. Run cold water over the pasta and set aside to cool.
7. In a large pot, heat the olive oil and sauté the onions until softened, 3 minutes. Stir in the garlic and cook until fragrant, 30 seconds.
8. Stir in the tomato paste, tomatoes, saffron, and cinnamon sticks; cook for 2 minutes and then mix in the chicken broth, salt, and black pepper.
9. Simmer for 20 to 25 minutes while you make the meatballs.
10. In a large bowl, mix the pork rinds, beef, egg, almond milk, garlic, salt, black pepper,

coriander, nutmeg powder, paprika, ginger paste, cumin powder, cayenne pepper, turmeric powder, cloves powder, cilantro, parsley, 3 tablespoons of scallions, and almond flour. Form 1-inch meatballs from the mixture.

11. Heat olive oil in a skillet and fry the meatballs until brown on all sides, 10 minutes.
12. Put meatballs into the sauce, coat well with the sauce and continue cooking for 10 minutes.
13. Divide the pasta onto serving plates and spoon the meatballs with sauce on top. Garnish with the feta cheese, remaining scallions and serve warm.

Thai Beef Shirataki Stir-Fry

Ingredients:

- 4 garlic cloves, minced
- 1 ½ cups fresh Thai basil leaves
- 2 tbsp toasted sesame seeds
- 1 tbsp chopped peanuts
- 1 tbsp chopped fresh scallions
- 3 tbsp coconut aminos
- 2 tbsp fish sauce
- 2 (8 oz) packs angel hair shirataki
- 2 tbsp olive oil, divided
- 1 ¼ lb flank steak, cut into bite-size pieces
- Salt and black pepper to taste

- 1 white onion, thinly sliced
- 1 red bell pepper, deseeded and sliced
- 1 cup sliced shiitake mushrooms
- 1 tbsp hot sauce

Directions:

1. Boil 2 cups of water in a medium pot over medium heat.
2. Strain the shirataki pasta through a colander and rinse very well under hot running water.
3. Allow proper draining and pour the shirataki pasta into the boiling water. Cook for 3 minutes and strain again.
4. Place a dry skillet over medium heat and stir-fry the shirataki pasta until visibly dry, and makes a squeaky sound when stirred, 1 to 2 minutes. Take off the heat and set aside.
5. Heat the olive oil in a large skillet, season the meat with salt, black pepper, and sear in the

oil on both sides until brown, 5 minutes. Transfer to a plate and set aside.
6. Add onion, bell pepper, and mushrooms to the skillet; cook for 5 minutes. Stir in the garlic and cook until fragrant, 1 minute. Return the beef to the skillet and add the pasta.
7. Quickly, combine the sauce's Ingredients: in a small bowl: coconut aminos, fish sauce, and hot sauce. Pour the mixture over the beef mix.
8. Top with the Thai basil and toss well to coat. Cook for 1 to 2 minutes or until warmed through.
9. Dish the food onto serving plates and garnish with the sesame seeds, peanuts, and scallions.

Cauliflower Crust Pizza

Ingredients:

For the base

- 1 cauliflower (about 750g/1lb 10oz)
- 100g ground almonds
- 2 eggs, beaten
- 1 tbsp dried oregano

For the topping

- 2 tbsp olive oil, plus extra for greasing
- 1 small red onion, cut into 8 wedges
- ½ small bunch basil, leaves picked
- 125g ball mozzarella
- 25g Grana Padano or Parmesan (or vegetarian alternative), grated, plus extra to serve
- 227g can chopped tomatoes

- 1 tbsp tomato purée

- 1 garlic clove, crushed

- ½ large aubergine, thinly sliced lengthways into long strips

- a few pinches of chilli flakes

Directions:

1. Heat oven to 200C/180C fan/gas 6. Remove the leaves from the cauliflower and trim the stalk end, then cut into chunks.
2. Blitz half the cauliflower in a food processor until finely chopped, like rice. Transfer to a bowl and repeat with the remaining half.
3. Tip all the cauliflower in a bowl, cover with cling film and microwave on High for 5-6 mins until softened.
4. Tip onto a clean tea towel and leave to cool a little. Once cool enough to handle, scrunch up the tea towel and squeeze as much liquid as you can out of the cauliflower, then transfer

to a clean bowl. Stir in the ground almonds, egg, oregano and plenty of seasoning.
5. Line a baking tray with baking parchment and grease with oil. Mound the cauliflower mix into the centre of the tray, then use a spoon and your hands to spread out into a 30cm round.
6. Make it a little thicker at the edges to create a 'crust'. Bake for 15-18 mins until golden brown and starting to crisp a little at the edges.
7. Meanwhile, heat a griddle pan, brush each aubergine slice on both sides with a little of the oil, season and cook for 5-6 mins, turning once, until softened and charred you'll need to do this in batches. Transfer to a plate.
8. Brush the onions with oil, season and griddle for 5-8 mins until softened and charred. To make the tomato sauce, whizz the canned

tomatoes, tomato purée, garlic and some seasoning in a blender until smooth.
9. Transfer to a small saucepan, bring to a simmer and cook gently for 8-10 mins until thick (you don't want any watery tomato soaking into the cauliflower base). Tear half the basil leaves and stir through the sauce.
10. Once the cauliflower base is cooked, set aside to cool a little. Turn the oven up to 240C/220C fan/gas 8. Drain the mozzarella and pat dry with kitchen paper.
11. Spread the tomato sauce over the base, sprinkle over the Grana Padano, then arrange the aubergines, red onion and mozzarella on top.
12. Scatter over the chilli flakes and return to the oven for 10-12 mins. Before serving, shave over a little more cheese and scatter with the remaining basil leaves.

Spelt Pizza Bianco With Jersey Royals

Ingredients:

For the biga

- 75g spelt flour
- 75g plain flour, plus extra for dusting
- ½ tsp fast-action dried yeast
- ½ tsp caster sugar

For the final dough

- 150g spelt flour
- 125g wholemeal flour
- 1 tsp fast-action dried yeast
- 2 tbsp olive oil

For the topping

- 6 Jersey Royal potatoes
- 4 thyme sprigs, leaves picked

- 2 tbsp extra virgin olive oil
- 1 garlic clove, crushed
- 75g crème fraîche

For the mint & watercress pistou

- ½ small pack fresh mint, leaves picked, plus extra to serve
- 25g pack watercress, washed
- 2 tbsp extra virgin olive oil
- 1 tsp red wine vinegar

Directions:

1. Make the biga the night before. Mix the two flours, yeast and sugar in a bowl. Slowly add 150ml lukewarm water and stir to create a thick batter.
2. Cover with a plastic carrier bag or dry tea towel and leave in a warm place overnight to ferment.

3. The next day, add the other flours, yeast, olive oil and 1 tsp salt to the biga, then gradually mix in enough water to make a soft, wet dough that still holds its shape (we used 200-220ml). Cover and leave to rise for 2-4 hrs or until tripled in size.
4. Once the dough has risen, punch the dough to knock the air out, then tip out onto a heavily floured surface. Knead in the flour until the dough stops sticking to your hands it should be very soft and springy, but not so wet that it sticks to the surface.
5. Divide the dough into two balls. Roll one out to make a large pizza base approx 1cm thick (or divide in half again to make two smaller pizzas).
6. The other ball should be frozen for use at a later date. Heat oven to 210C/ 190C fan/gas 61/2 . Transfer the base to an oiled baking

sheet and prove for 5 mins while you prepare the toppings.
7. Using a mandolin or sharp knife, slice the potatoes very thinly. Pat away any excess moisture with a clean tea towel. In a bowl, toss the potato slices and thyme leaves in the olive oil and season.
8. In another bowl, mix the garlic and crème fraîche, then spread onto the pizza base with the back of a spoon.
9. Lay the potato slices on top and drizzle with any remaining olive oil or thyme from the bowl. Bake for 15-20 mins until the base is puffed and golden and the potatoes are crisping up around the edges.
10. Meanwhile, make the pistou by blitzing all the Ingredients: in a food processor. To serve, drizzle the pistou over the pizza and scatter over some mint leaves.

The Super Gluten Free Pizza Crust + Sauce

Ingredients:

- 1/2 tsp baking powder
- 3 tbsp (37 g) sugar, divided
- 1 tbsp (10 g) yeast
- 1 1/4 cup (200 ml) warm water, divided
- 3 cups (440 g) gluten free flour blend (1 cup (160 g) white rice flour + 1 cup (160 g) brown rice flour + 1 cup (120 g) tapioca flour + 3/4 tsp xanthan gum)
- 1 tsp salt
- 1 tbsp (15 ml) olive oil

Directions:

1. Preheat oven to 350 degrees F (176 C).

2. In a small bowl, combine yeast and 3/4 cup (180 ml) warm water - about 110 degrees F (43 C).
3. Too hot and it will kill the yeast! Let set for 5 minutes to activate. Sprinkle in 1 Tbsp (12 g) of the sugar a few minutes in.
4. In a separate bowl, combine gluten free flour blend, salt, baking powder and remaining 2 Tbsp (25 g) sugar. Whisk until well combined.
5. Make a well in the dry mixture and add the yeast mixture. Add the olive oil and additional 1/2 cup (120 ml) warm water before stirring.
6. Then stir it all together until well combined, using a wooden spoon (see photo).
7. Lightly coat a baking sheet or pizza stone with non-stick spray and plop your dough down.
8. Using your hands and a little brown rice flour if it gets too sticky, work from the middle and push to spread/flatten the dough out to the

edge (see pictures). You want it to be pretty thin - less than 1/4 inch.

9. Put the pizza in the oven to pre-bake for roughly 25-30 minutes, or until it begins to look dry. Cracks may appear, but that's normal and totally OK.
10. Remove from oven and spread generously with your favorite pizza sauce, cheese and desired toppings. We went with Daiya to keep ours dairy-free. Pop back in oven for another 20-25 minutes, or until the crust edge looks golden brown and the toppings are warm and bubbly.
11. Cut immediately and serve. Reheats well the next day in the oven or microwave.

Gluten Free Pizza Power

Ingredients:

For tomato sauce

- 1/2 teaspoon fine sea salt
- 1/4 teaspoon dried oregano
- 1 (15-ounce) can crushed tomatoes with added purée
- 4 1/2 teaspoons extra-virgin olive oil
- 1/2 teaspoon sugar

For pizza crust

- 1/2 cup whole milk
- 2 1/4 teaspoons active dry yeast, from 1 (1/4-ounce) package
- 2 teaspoons sugar
- 2 large egg whites, lightly beaten

- 3 tablespoons plus 1 teaspoon extra-virgin olive oil
- 3/4 cup tapioca flour
- 1/2 cup white rice flour*
- 1/3 cup chickpea flour
- 1/3 cup sorghum flour
- 1 teaspoon xanthum gum
- 1 teaspoon fine sea salt

For topping

- 4 teaspoons extra-virgin olive oil
- 8 ounces fresh mozzarella, coarsely grated (about 1 1/2 cups)
- 1/4 ounce parmigiano-reggiano, finely grated (about 1 tablespoon)
- 4 large fresh basil leaves, roughly torn

- *be sure to use white rice flour; brown will result in gritty pizza dough.

    stone or heavy baking sheet, baking peel or heavy baking sheet, parchment paper

Directions:

Make tomato sauce

1. In a 4-quart nonreactive saucepan over very low heat, stir together tomatoes and oil. Bring to simmer, cover partially, and continue simmering, stirring occasionally, until sauce is reduced to 1 cup, 20 to 25 minutes. Stir in sugar, salt, and oregano, cover. Keep warm or refrigerate, covered, up to 5 days.

Make pizza crust

2. In bowl of electric mixer, whisk together tapioca flour, white rice flour, chickpea flour, sorghum flour, xanthum gum, and salt.

3. In small saucepan over moderate heat, stir together milk and 1/4 cup water and heat until warm but not hot to the touch, about 1

minute (the mixture should register between 105°F and 115° F on candy thermometer). Stir in yeast and sugar. Add milkyeast mixture, egg whites, and 2 tablespoons oil to dry Ingredients: and, using paddle attachment, beat at medium speed, scraping bowl occasionally, until dough is very smooth and very thick, about 5 minutes.

4. Remove racks from oven, set pizza stone or heavy upturned baking sheet on bottom of oven, and preheat to 400°F. (Preheat at least 45 minutes if using pizza stone or 20 minutes if using baking sheet.)
5. Have ready two 12-inch squares parchment paper. Scrape half of dough onto each square and form each half into a ball.
6. Coat each ball with 2 teaspoons oil, then use oiled fingertips to pat and stretch each ball into 9-inch-diameter round, 1/4 inch thick, with a 1/2-inch-thick border. Loosely cover

rounds with plastic wrap and let rise in warm draft-free place until each pizza is about 10 inches in diameter, about 20 minutes.

7. Using baking peel, transfer 1 crust with parchment to preheated pizza stone and bake until top is puffed and firm and underside is crisp, 5 to 10 minutes. Using baking peel and discarding parchment paper, transfer baked crust to rack to cool.

8. Bake second crust in same manner. (Baked crusts can be made ahead and frozen, wrapped in plastic wrap, up to 1 month. Thaw in 350°F oven until hot, 4 to 5 minutes, before topping and broiling.)

Top and broil pizzas

9. Preheat broiler. Transfer baked crusts to 2 large baking sheets. Brush 1 teaspoon olive oil over each crust. Spread each with sauce, leaving 1/2-inch border bare, then sprinkle each with mozzarella and Parmigiano-

Reggiano. Drizzle remaining 2 teaspoons olive oil over pizzas.

10. Broil pizzas about 4 inches from heat, rotating as needed for even browning, until cheese is bubbling and browned in places and crust is golden brown, 4 to 8 minutes. Scatter with basil, slice, and serve immediately.

Kale-Artichoke Pizza

Ingredients:

For the crust:

- 1 egg, beaten
- 1 tsp Italian seasoning
- ½ tsp garlic powder
- ½ cup almond flour
- 1 ½ cups grated mozzarella cheese
- 2 tbsp cream cheese

For the topping:

- ½ tsp garlic powder
- ¼ cup grated Parmesan cheese
- ½ cup grated Mozzarella cheese
- Salt and black pepper to taste

- 4 tbsp cream cheese, room temperature
- ½ cup chopped kale
- ¼ cup chopped artichoke
- 1 lemon, juiced

Directions:

1. Preheat the oven to 425 F and line a pizza pan with parchment paper.
2. In a medium safe-microwave bowl, combine the mozzarella and cream cheese. Melt in the microwave for 30 seconds to 1 minute.
3. Remove the bowl from the oven and mix in the egg, Italian seasoning, garlic powder, and almond flour.
4. Spread the mixture on the pizza pan and bake in the oven for 15 minutes or until crusty. Remove the crust from the oven and set aside to cool.
5. In a medium bowl, mix the cream cheese, kale, artichoke, lemon juice, garlic powder,

Parmesan cheese, mozzarella cheese, salt, and black pepper. Spread the mixture on the crust and bake again for 15 minutes or slightly golden.

Sausage-Pepper Pizza Coconut Tuna Zucchini Bake

Ingredients:

- 2 cups coconut milk
- 4 medium zucchinis, spiralized
- 1 cup grated Parmesan cheese
- 1 (15 oz) can tuna in water, drained and flaked
- 1 tbsp butter
- 1 cup green beans, chopped
- 1 bunch asparagus, trimmed and cut into 1-inch pieces
- 2 tbsp arrowroot starch
- Salt and black pepper to taste

Directions:

1. Preheat the oven to 380 F.

2. Melt the butter in a medium skillet and sauté the green beans and asparagus until softened, about 5 minutes. Set aside.
3. In a medium saucepan, mix the arrowroot starch with the coconut milk. Bring to a boil over medium heat with frequent stirring until thickened, 3 minutes. Stir in half of the Parmesan cheese until melted.
4. Mix in the green beans, asparagus, zucchinis and tuna. Season with salt and black pepper.
5. Transfer the mixture to a baking dish and cover the top with the remaining Parmesan cheese.
6. Bake in the oven until the cheese melts and golden on top, 20 minutes.
7. Remove the food from the oven and serve warm.

Creamy Garlic Shrimp With Angel Hair

Ingredients:

For the shrimp sauce:

- 1 ½ cups heavy cream
- ½ cup grated Asiago cheese
- 2 tbsp chopped fresh parsley
- 1 tbsp olive oil
- 1 lb shrimp, peeled and deveined
- Salt and black pepper to taste
- 2 tbsp unsalted butter
- 6 garlic cloves, minced
- ½ cup dry white wine

For the angel hair shirataki:

- 2 (8 oz) packs angel hair shirataki noodles
- Salt to season

Directions:

For the shrimp sauce:

1. Heat the olive oil in a large skillet, season the shrimp with salt and black pepper, and cook in the oil on both sides until pink and opaque, 2 minutes. Set aside.
2. Melt the butter in the skillet and sauté the garlic until fragrant. Stir in the white wine and cook until reduced by half, meanwhile, scraping the bottom of the pan to deglaze.
3. Reduce the heat to low and stir in the heavy cream. Allow simmering for 1 minute and stir in the Asiago cheese to melt. Return the shrimp to the sauce and sprinkle the parsley on top. Adjust the taste with salt and black pepper, if needed.

For the angel hair shirataki:

4. Bring 2 cups of water to a boil in a pot. Strain the shirataki pasta through a colander and rinse very well under hot running water.

5. Allow proper draining and pour the shirataki pasta into the boiling water. Take off the heat, let sit for 3 minutes and strain again.
6. Place a dry skillet over medium heat and stir-fry the shirataki pasta until visibly dry and makes a squeaky sound when stirred, 1 to 2 minutes. Season with salt and plate. Top the shirataki pasta with the shrimp sauce and serve warm.

Parsnip Soup

INGREDIENTS:

- ½ cup all-purpose flour
- ¼ tsp salt
- ¼ tsp pepper
- 1 can vegetable broth
- 1 tablespoon olive oil
- 1 cup parsnip
- ¼ red onion
- 1 cup heavy cream

DIRECTIONS:

1. In a saucepan heat olive oil and sauté parsnip until tender
2. Add remaining Ingredients: to the saucepan and bring to a boil

3. When all the vegetables are tender transfer to a blender and blend until smooth
4. Pour soup into bowls, garnish with parsley and serve

Spinach Soup

INGREDIENTS:

- ½ cup all-purpose flour
- ¼ tsp salt
- ¼ tsp pepper
- 1 can vegetable broth
- 1 tablespoon olive oil
- 1 lb. spinach
- ¼ red onion
- 1 cup heavy cream

DIRECTIONS:

1. In a saucepan heat olive oil and sauté spinach until tender
2. Add remaining Ingredients: to the saucepan and bring to a boil

3. When all the vegetables are tender transfer to a blender and blend until smooth
4. Pour soup into bowls, garnish with parsley and serve

Almond Skillet Bread

Ingredients:

- ½ cup + 1 tablespoon butter
- ½ cup flax seed meal
- ¾ cup almond milk
- 2 teaspoon baking powder
- 3 big eggs
- 2 cups almond flour
- 1 ½ cups Cheddar cheese, shredded
- Salt to taste

Directions:

1. Start by turning your oven to 425F to preheat it. Use a heatproof skillet and add one tablespoon of butter. Insert it into the oven.
2. Grab a big bowl and add flax seed meal, almond flour, one cup of cheddar cheese,

baking powder, and salt to taste (you shouldn't need more than ½ teaspoon). Combine all the Ingredients: well.

3. Take a separate bowl and lightly beat the eggs. Add them to the flour mixture along with almond milk and ½ cup of melted butter. Stir everything until you combine the Ingredients: well.
4. Transfer the dough to the skillet and even out the top with a spoon.
5. Use the remaining cheddar cheese to sprinkle over the bread. Bake for 15 minutes at the set temperature. Allow it to cool down before serving.

Just-Like-Regular Keto Bread

Ingredients:

- 1 teaspoon baking powder
- ½ teaspoon xanthan gum
- 2 tablespoons coconut oil
- ½ cup melted butter
- 8 medium eggs
- 2 cup almond flour
- ½ teaspoon salt

Directions:

1. Start by turning your oven to 350F to preheat it. Grab a bowl and add an egg to it. Use an electric hand mixer to beat the eggs for no more than 2 minutes.
2. Add melted butter and coconut oil and continue until you thoroughly mix everything.

3. Add almond flour, baking powder, xanthan gum, and salt to taste (you don't need more than ½ teaspoon). Combine everything well until you get a pretty thick batter.
4. Transfer the batter into a loaf pan you previously greased with cooking spray and lined with parchment paper. Bake for 40 minutes at the set temperature or until the toothpick comes out clean.

Peanut Flour Bread

Ingredients:

- 2 tablespoons Erythritol or sweetener of your choice
- 4 tablespoons melted butter
- 1 teaspoon vanilla
- 1 teaspoon baking powder
- 4 big egg yolks
- 5 ounces cream cheese
- ½ cup peanut flour
- Salt to taste

Directions:

1. Start by turning your oven to 350F to preheat it. Use parchment paper to line a loaf pan.
2. Grab a bowl and add cream cheese and melted butter to it.

3. Use an electric hand mixer to combine everything well. Add Erythritol or sweetener of your choice, baking powder, vanilla, egg yolks, and salt.
4. Mix everything well until the Ingredients: are thoroughly combined.
5. Stir in the peanut flour and mix until thick batter forms. Transfer it to the loaf pan and even out the top. Bake for 25 minutes at the set temperature.

Apple Goat Cheese And Pecan Pizza

Ingredients:

- teaspoons chopped fresh thyme
- tablespoon extra-virgin olive oil
- teaspoons Dijon mustard
- teaspoon fresh lemon juice
- 1/2 teaspoons honey
- cups baby arugula
- (1-pound) six-grain pizza crust
- Cooking spray
- cups thinly sliced Fuji apple (about 8 ounces)
- cup (4 ounces) crumbled goat cheese
- tablespoons chopped pecans, toasted

Directions:

1. Preheat oven to 450°.
2. Place pizza crust on a baking sheet coated with cooking spray. Arrange apple slices evenly over pizza crust; top with cheese.
3. Sprinkle thyme evenly over cheese. Bake at 450° for 8 minutes or until cheese melts and begins to brown.
4. Combine oil and next 3 Ingredients: (through honey) in a medium bowl, stirring with a whisk. Add arugula; toss gently to coat.
5. Sprinkle pecans evenly over pizza; top with arugula mixture. Cut pizza into 6 wedges.

Apple Walnut Pizza With Caramelized Onions

Ingredients:

- 1/2 cups (6 ounces) shredded Cheddar cheese

- cup (4 ounces) crumbled Gorgonzola cheese, divided

- 2 recipe Brick Oven Pizza Dough
- large Granny Smith apple, cored and thinly sliced
- tablespoon extra virgin olive oil
- large red onion, thinly sliced
- tablespoons balsamic vinegar
- 2 cup coarsely chopped walnuts

Directions:

1. Heat oil in a small saucepan over medium-high heat; stir in onion and balsamic vinegar. Reduce heat to medium-low, and cook for about 15 minutes or until onions are caramelized; let cool.
2. Sprinkle Cheddar and 1/2 cup Gorgonzola cheese evenly over prepared pizza dough; top evenly with onion mixture. Arrange apple over onion mixture; top with remaining Gorgonzola. sprinkle with walnuts.

3. Bake at 500° for 5 to 7 minutes or until browned and bubbly.

Artichoke Pizzas With Lemony Green Bean Salad

Ingredients:

- 4 cup roasted almonds, chopped
- 1/2 cups shredded Cheddar (6 ounces)
- 2 teaspoon dried oregano
- 9-ounce package frozen French-cut green beans, thawed
- tablespoons fresh lemon juice
- pita breads, split horizontally
- tablespoons extra-virgin olive oil
- 12-ounce jar roasted red peppers, drained and sliced
- 6-ounce jar artichokes, drained and cut in half
- Kosher salt and pepper

Directions:

1. Heat broiler. Arrange the pita halves cut-side up on a broiler proof sheet pan. Drizzle with 2 tablespoons of the oil and broil until crisp, 2 to 3 minutes.
2. Top with the red peppers, artichokes, almonds, Cheddar, and oregano. Broil until the cheese has melted, 2 to 3 minutes.
3. Divide the green beans among bowls. Drizzle with the lemon juice and the remaining 1 tablespoon of oil.
4. Season with 1/4 teaspoon salt and 1/8 teaspoon pepper. Serve with the pizzas.

Beefed Up Pizza Wedges With Pepperoni And Black Olives

Ingredients:

- Sliced mushrooms
- 1 tsp Italian spice
- blend Sliced dark
- olives 1/4 tsp pepper
- 1/4 tsp garlic powder
- Green chime pepper
- Sliced pepperoni
- Red onion
- 1 lb. ground beef
- 1/4 tsp onion powder
- Tomato sauce

- 1 lb. new Italian wiener

- 1/4 tsp salt

Directions:

1. Preheat your stove to 450 degrees F.
2. In a little bowl, join pepper, onion powder, salt, ground hamburger, and garlic powder.
3. Divide the hamburger combination and spot them into 2 round cake container that were fixed with material paper.
4. Pat the meat in the cake dish and spread them like pizza dough.
5. Thinly spread a layer of pureed tomatoes on top of the patty and top it with ringer pepper, mushroom, pepperoni and olives.
6. Place the cake skillet in the broiler and prepare them for around 20 minutes.
7. Slice into wedges and serve while they are hot.

Beef Paleo Pizza With Portobello Mushrooms

Ingredients:

- 4 enormous Portobello mushroom
- covers 1/2 cup Water
- 1 lb. ground beef
- Lettuce Tomato
- 1/4 cup Taco Sauce
- 2 Tbsp Taco Seasoning
- Olives Zucchini

Directions:

1. Preheat your stove to 400 F.
2. In a baking sheet, line the mushrooms and brush them with pepper, salt and olive oil.
3. Bake the mushrooms for around ten minutes then, at that point, flip the cuts on converse

to cook the opposite side; prepare for another 10 minutes.
4. In a skillet, cook the hamburger over medium hotness; add water and Taco seasoning.
5. Keep on blending to thicken the taco sauce and completely cook the meat.

   6. Pour the taco sauce on every one of the mushroom cuts and top it with cooked ground beef.
6. Serve the No-Crust Beef Paleo Pizza with Portobello Mushrooms with any of the suggested garnishes like Tomato, zucchini, lettuce or olives.

Wild Rockets, Bacon And Mushroom Paleo Pizza

Ingredients:

for the Pizza Crust

- 3 eggs (confine free)
- 1/2 teaspoon basil
- 1/4 teaspoon ground cumin
- 1/2 teaspoon baking soft drink
- 2 cloves garlic
- 1 cup coconut milk
- 1/2 cup coconut flour

for the Toppings

- 4 Bacon strips
- Wild rocket
- Chipotle powder

- Rhubarb-Orange Compote 8

- Button mushrooms

Directions:

1. Preheat your broiler to 350 degrees F.
2. Drizzle olive oil on a material paper and spot it on a pizza pan.
3. In a food processor, blend all fixings and set it on beat until the combination becomes batter like.
4. Use a spatula to place the batter blend in the material paper and cover all edges of the pan.
5. Bake the batter blend for 15 minutes.
6. For the fixings, add the powdered chipotle and Rhubarb Orange Compote to the pizza dough.
7. For the second layer of fixing, add bacon and mushrooms prior to baking it for 8 minutes.
8. Wait until the outside becomes brilliant brown to include the wild rockets top.
9. Slice into quarters and serve while hot.

Beef Ragu With Veggie Pasta

Ingredients:

- 1/4 cup sugar-free tomato sauce
- 4 tbsp chopped fresh parsley + extra for garnishing
- 4 green bell peppers, spiralized
- 4 red bell peppers, spiralized
- 1 small red onion, spiralized
- 2 tbsp butter
- 1 lb ground beef
- Salt and black pepper to taste
- 1 cup grated Parmesan cheese

Directions:

1. Heat half of the butter in a medium skillet and cook the beef until brown, 5 minutes. Season with salt and black pepper.
2. Stir in the tomato sauce, parsley, and cook for 10 minutes or until the sauce reduces by a quarter.
3. Stir in the bell pepper and onion noodles; cook for 1 minute and turn the heat off.
4. Adjust the taste with salt, black pepper, and dish the food onto serving plates. Garnish with the Parmesan cheese and more parsley; serve warm.

Classic Beef Lasagna

Ingredients:

For the lasagna noodles:

- 1 ½ cup grated mozzarella cheese
- 1 tsp dried Italian seasoning
- 4 oz cream cheese, room temperature
- 2 large eggs, cracked into a bowl

For the lasagna filling:

- 1 cup sugar-free marinara sauce
- 6 tbsp ricotta cheese
- ½ cup grated mozzarella cheese
- ½ cup grated Parmesan cheese
- 1 lb ground beef
- 1 medium white onion, chopped

- 1 tsp Italian seasoning

- Salt and black pepper to taste

Directions:

For the lasagna noodles:

1. Preheat the oven to 350 F and line a 9 x 13 inch baking sheet with parchment paper.
2. In a food processor, add cream cheese, mozzarella cheese, Italian seasoning, and eggs.
3. Blend until well mixed. Pour the cheese mixture on the baking sheet and spread across the pan. Bake until set and firm to touch, 20 minutes. Remove and let cool.

For the lasagna sauce:

4. In a large skillet, combine the beef, onion and cook until brown, 5 minutes. Season with the Italian seasoning, salt, and black pepper. Cook further for 1 minute and mix in the marinara sauce. Simmer for 3 minutes. Turn the heat off.

5. 2. Evenly cut the lasagna pasta into thirds making sure it fits into your baking sheet.
6. Spread a layer of the beef mixture in the baking sheet and make a first single layer on the beef mixture.
7. Spread a third of the remaining beef mixture on the pasta, top with a third each of the ricotta cheese, mozzarella cheese, and Parmesan cheese.
8. Repeat the layering two more times using the remaining Ingredients: in the same quantities.
9. Bake in the oven until the cheese melts and is bubbly with the sauce, 20 minutes
10. Remove the lasagna, allow cooling for 2 minutes and dish onto serving plates. Serve warm.

Creamy Sun-Dried & Parsnip Noodles

Ingredients:

- 1 ¼ cup heavy cream
- 1 cup shaved Parmesan cheese
- ¼ tsp dried basil
- ¼ tsp red chili flakes
- 2 tbsp chopped fresh parsley for garnishing
- 3 tbsp butter
- 1 lb beef stew meat, cut into strips
- Salt and black pepper to taste
- 4 large parsnips, spiralized
- 1 cup sun dried tomatoes in oil, chopped
- 4 garlic cloves, minced

Directions:

1. Melt 1 tablespoon of butter in a large skillet, season the beef with salt, black pepper and cook in the butter until brown, and cooked within, 8 to 10 minutes.
2. In another medium skillet, melt the remaining butter and sauté the parsnips until softened, 5 to 7 minutes. Set aside.
3. Stir in the sun-dried tomatoes and garlic into the beef, cook until fragrant, 1 minute.
4. Reduce the heat to low and stir in the heavy cream and Parmesan cheese. Simmer until the cheese melts. Season with the salt, basil, and red chili flakes.
5. Fold in the parsnips until well coated and cook for 2 more minutes.
6. Dish the food into serving plates, garnish with the parsley and serve warm.

No Yeast Pizza Dough

Ingredients:

- 1 tsp salt

- 1 tbsp oil

- 350g plain flour

- 2 ¾ tsp baking powder

- Additional toppings of your choice

Directions:

1. Heat the oven to 200C/180C fan/gas 6.
2. Mix together 350g flour, 2 ¾ tsp baking powder and 1 tsp salt in a small bowl, add 1 tbsp oil and 170ml water then stir until it forms a ball. If stiff, add more water, it should be soft but not sticky.
3. Knead on a floured surface for 3-4 mins. Roll into 2 balls, then flatten out.
4. Add toppings and bake each on a baking sheet for 15 mins.

Rainbow Pizzas

Ingredients:

- 8 green olives, pitted and halved (optional)
- 150g mozzarella cherries (bocconcini)
- 2 tbsp fresh pesto
- handful fresh basil leaves, to serve
- 2 plain pizza bases
- 6 tbsp passata
- 400g mixed red and yellow tomatoes, sliced
- 75g sprouting broccoli, stems finely sliced

Directions:

1. Heat the oven to 180C/160C fan/gas 4. Put each pizza base on a baking sheet and spread each with half of the passata.

2. Arrange the tomatoes on the top in rings or wedges of colour and add the broccoli and the olives, if using.
3. Squish the mozzarella cherries (bocconcini) a little before dotting them over the pizzas, then drizzle 1 tbsp pesto over each.
4. Bake for 15-20 mins or until the top is bubbling and just starting to brown a little. Scatter over the basil leaves before serving.

Pumpkin Pizza With Zucchini And Nuts

Ingredients:

- 1 tbsp psyllium seed husks
- 1 tbsp flax seeds
- 6 tbsp water
- 1 tbsp oregano
- 1 small butternut squash (about 600g)
- 1 small zucchini
- 1 cup of ground almond
- 1/2 cup of ground hazelnut
- 1/2 cup of chickpea flour
- 1 tbsp chia seeds
- Salt, pepper

Directions:

1. Start by making some pumpkin puree. I recommend you to bake it instead of cooking, so you'll need less flour. I baked my halved butternut squash for an hour at 200°C.
2. Mix the chia seeds, the psyllium seed husks and the flax seeds with 6 tbsp water. Let it set for 15 minutes. It will form a very thick mixture.
3. Scoop out the pumpkin flesh and add to a bowl with the shredded zucchini, the almond, the hazelnut, the chickpea flour the spices and the soaked seeds and mix it all together until it becomes a dough.
4. You can add a bit more of (chickpea) flour if the dough is not thick enough.
5. Put a baking paper in a pizza baking form or on a baking tray, grease it with a drop of olive oil and spread the mixture. I got two 30 cm pizzas with roughly 1 cm thick dough.

6. Bake for 30 minutes at 180°C, add your sauce and toppings, and put back in the oven for 5 more minutes. Enjoy!

Gluten-Free Pizza With Fresh Mozzarella, Olives, Basil, And Anaheim Peppers

Ingredients:

- 6 basil leaves, roughly torn

- 1/8 c. sliced Mediterranean-style black or green olives

- 1/2 Anaheim pepper, thinly sliced crosswise

- 1 Tbsp. grated Parmigiano-Reggiano cheese (optional)

- Olive oil for drizzling on top of the pizza

- 1/2 lb. (orange-size portion) Gluten-Free Pizza Crust (above)

- 1/2 c. canned Italian-style chopped tomatoes, well-drained by draining through a strainer, or use any prepared tomato sauce you like

- 1/4 lb. sliced fresh mozzarella cheese, buffalo-milk variety if available

- White or brown rice flour for dusting

Directions:

1. Thirty minutes before baking time, preheat the oven to 500 degrees F, with a baking stone placed on the middle rack. Prepare and measure all the toppings in advance.

2. Dust the surface of the refrigerated dough with rice flour and cut off a 1/2-pound (orange-size) piece. Dust the piece with more rice flour and quickly shape it into a ball; this dough isn't stretched because there is no gluten in it just press it into the shape of a ball.

3. You will need to use lots of rice flour to prevent the dough from sticking to your hands or the work surface, but avoid working lumps of flour into the dough.

4. Sprinkle rice flour onto a 14-inch square piece of parchment paper.
5. Flatten the dough with your hands into an even circle, sprinkle generously with more rice flour, cover with a 14-inch piece of plastic wrap, then roll the dough between the parchment and plastic wrap to produce a 1/16- to 1/8-inch-thick round. Peel away the plastic wrap, leaving the crust on the parchment paper
6. Distribute a thin layer of tomatoes over the surface of the dough.
7. Scatter the mozzarella over the surface of the dough, then the basil, olives, pepper, and Parmigiano-Reggiano, if desired. Drizzle the pizza with about a teaspoon of olive oil. No further resting is needed prior to baking.
8. Slide the pizza and parchment directly onto the stone. Check for doneness in 10-12 minutes.

9. Take a peek at the bottom of the crust if you'd like it to be browner, slide the pizza and parchment off the stone and directly onto the oven rack for a couple of minutes.
(Parchment paper will turn black, which is fine.) Allow the pizza to cool slightly on a rack before serving, to allow the cheese to set.

Gluten-Free Tuscan-Style Pizza

Ingredients:

For the gluten-free pizza base dough:

- 2 level tsp gluten-free yeast

- 40g (just under 1 1/2 oz) whole egg replacer (or 2 medium eggs)

- 300ml (1/2 pint) unsweetened soya milk

- 1tsp cider vinegar

- 4tbsp olive oil

- 450g (15oz) gluten-free white bread flour

- 2 level tbsp sugar

- 1 level tsp salt

For the pizza topping:

- 180g tub marinaded and grilled artichokes in oil, or similar product

- 3 slices Parma ham
- 30g (1oz) Cheddar-style cheese, coarsely grated
- A few sprigs of thyme or 1/2 teaspoon dried thyme
- 8 black olives, optional
- Large heavy baking sheet, lightly oiled
- 1 onion, peeled and chopped
- 1tbsp olive oil
- 1 fat clove garlic, peeled and chopped
- 1 small chilli, de-seeded and chopped, optional
- 400g can chopped tomatoes
- 2tbsp tomato ketchup
- Salt and ground black pepper

Directions:

1. To make the pizza base: Mix the flour, sugar, salt, yeast and egg replacer in the bowl of an electric mixer/food processor fitted with a dough hook, or use a large bowl.
2. Measure the milk into a jug and add 175ml (6fl oz) hot water (unless you are using eggs, then only add 2tbsp hot water and beat in the eggs), the cider vinegar and oil.
3. Pour this mixture into the dry Ingredients: and mix really well to make a soft, slightly sticky dough.
4. To make the pizza: Spoon the other half of the dough on to the baking sheet and spread to around about 25cm (10in) in diameter. Leave, uncovered, in a warm place to rise; allow about 30 mins.
5. Meanwhile, make the topping: Cook the onion in the oil in a frying pan for about 5 mins until softened.

6. Add the garlic and chilli, if using, then cook for another minute before stirring in the tomatoes, ketchup and seasoning. Simmer and let it thicken for 10-15 mins.
7. Leave in the pan to cool while the pizza base rises.
8. Set the oven to 220°C (425°F, gas mark 7).
9. Spread the tomato topping over the base to within about 1cm (½ in) of the edge.
10. Arrange halved artichoke hearts on top with strips of Parma ham, sprinkle with cheese, thyme leaves and olives, if using, and drizzle with the oil from the artichokes - about 1tbsp. Season well.
11. Bake for 10 mins near the bottom of the oven then turn the oven down to 200°C (400°F, gas mark 6) and cook for another 20 mins until really crisp on the bottom. Serve warm with salad.

Pepperoni Pizza

Ingredients:

- 1 teaspoon xanthan gum
- 1/4 teaspoon salt
- 2 tablespoons olive oil, divided
- 2 large egg whites
- 1 large egg
- 3/4 cup lower-sodium marinara sauce (such as Dell'Amore)
- 4 ounces part-skim mozzarella cheese, shredded (about 1 cup)
- 2 ounces sliced turkey pepperoni
- 2 tablespoons grated fresh Parmesan cheese
- 1/2 cup warm water (100° to 110°)

- 2 teaspoons granulated sugar
- 1 package dry yeast (about 2 1/4 teaspoons)
- ounces white rice flour (about 3/4 cup)
- 1.4 ounces sweet white sorghum flour (about 1/3 cup)
- 1.4 ounces tapioca flour (about 1/3 cup)
- 1.7 ounces potato starch (about 1/3 cup)
- 0.9 ounce flaxseed meal (about 1/4 cup)

Directions:
1. Combine 1/2 cup water, sugar, and yeast in a small bowl, stirring with a whisk. Let stand 5 minutes or until yeast mixture is bubbly.
2. Weigh or lightly spoon flours, potato starch, and flaxseed meal into dry measuring cups; level with a knife.

3. Combine flours, potato starch, flaxseed meal, xanthan gum, and salt in a large bowl; beat with a mixer at medium speed until blended.
4. Add yeast mixture, 1 tablespoon oil, egg whites, and egg; beat at low speed 1 minute or until combined. Increase speed to medium; beat 2 minutes.
5. Coat a baking sheet with 1 teaspoon oil. Scrape dough onto pan. Lightly coat hands with oil.
6. Press dough into a 14-inch circle, coating hands with oil as needed to prevent dough from sticking.
7. Coat top of dough with any remaining oil. Cover with plastic wrap, and let rise in a warm place (85°), free from drafts, for 30 minutes.
8. Preheat oven to 400°.
9. Remove plastic wrap, and bake crust at 400° for 17 minutes or until bottom lightly browns.

Cool completely. Increase oven temperature to 425°.

10. Spread marinara over crust, leaving a 1/2-inch border; top with mozzarella cheese, pepperoni, and Parmesan cheese. Bake at 425° for 16 minutes or until crust is golden and cheese melts.

Vegan Marguerite Pizza With Gluten-Free Crust

Ingredients:

Gluten-free pizza crust

- 1 teaspoon salt

- 1 teaspoon baking powder

- 1 3/4 cup Bob's Red Mill Gluten-Free 1-to1 Baking Blend, divided + extra for flouring your surface

- olive oil spray

- 3/4 cup water, heated to 110 F

- 2 1/2 teaspoons yeast

- 1 teaspoon sugar

- 1/2 cup aquafaba (chickpea brine)

- 2 tablespoons olive oil

Pizza sauce

- 1 teaspoon dried basil
- 1 teaspoon dried oregano
- 1/4 teaspoon garlic powder
- salt and pepper
- one 15-ounce can unsalted tomato sauce
- one 6-ounce can tomato paste
- 1/2 cup water
- 1 tablespoon olive oil

Toppings

- 2 to 3 tomatoes, sliced
- Macarella from But I Could Never Go Vegan! or a homemade cashew cheese sauce, or a store-bought vegan mozzarella
- fresh basil leaves

- red pepper flakes (optional)

Directions:

1. In a cup, combine the heated water, yeast and sugar. Stir gently to combine and then let sit and let the yeast activate for about 10 minutes.

2. In a large bowl, combine the brine, olive oil, salt, and baking powder. Once the yeast is fully activated, add the water/yeast mixture to the bowl and whisk to combine.

3. Add 1 cup of GF flour blend to the bowl and stir until just combined. Add a 1/2 cup of the flour and stir until combined. Add 1/4 cup of flour and stir until combined. The mixture should hold together without sticking to your fingers, but still be wet and sticky to the touch. If it's too sticky (sticking to your fingers), add flour by the tablespoon until the correct texture is achieved. If it's too dry (not wet/sticky to the touch), add water by the

tablespoon until the correct texture is achieved.

4. Place the ball of dough in a bowl sprayed lightly with olive oil (or pick the ball up and spray the inside of the bowl you've been working in with oil). Cover the bowl with a kitchen towel damped with warm water. Place the bowl in a warm, draft-free area and let the dough rise for 1 hour.

5. While the dough is rising, make the sauce. In a medium pot, combine the sauce Ingredients: and bring to a boil. Reduce the heat to a slow simmer and let simmer, stirring occasionally, for about 15 to 20 minutes. Remove from the heat and set aside.

6. Preheat the oven to 450 F. If using a pizza pan or baking sheet, get it out and lightly spray it with olive oil. Lay your tomato slices out on a couple sheets of paper towel. Sprinkle them

lightly with salt and pepper. Let them rest until ready to use.
7. If using a pizza stone, make sure it is in the oven as soon as you start preheating it.
8. Once the dough has risen, turn it out onto a floured surface. Roll the ball around in the flour and knead until the dough it tougher, softer, and more pliable. Pat the dough into a disc, flip and pat the disc a bit until it is a slightly larger disc. Continue flipping and patting until you have a 10 to 11-inch pizza crust. Transfer the crust to your pan/stone, spray the crust, particularly the edges, with olive oil, and bake for 10 minutes.
9. Remove the crust from the oven and spread pizza sauce over the top, leaving an inch around the edge clear. Top with sliced tomatoes and Macarella or vegan cheese of your choice. Return the pizza to the oven and let bake for another 7 to 10 minutes or until

the crust is fully risen and golden, and the cheese has melted and/or browned. Remove from the oven, top with basil leaves and red pepper flakes (if using), slice, and serve immediately.

Creamy Salmon Shirataki Fettucine

Ingredients:

For the shirataki fettuccine:

- 2 (8 oz) packs shirataki fettuccine

For the creamy salmon sauce:

- 3 garlic cloves, minced

- 1 ¼ cups heavy cream

- ½ cup dry white wine

- 1 tsp grated lemon zest

- 1 cup baby spinach

- 5 tbsp butter

- 4 salmon fillets, cut into 2-inch cubes

- Salt and black pepper to taste

- Lemon wedges for garnishing

Directions:

For the shirataki fettuccine:

1. Boil 2 cups of water in a pot over medium heat. Strain the shirataki pasta through a colander and rinse very well under hot running water. Pour the shirataki pasta into the boiling water. Take off the heat, let sit for 3 minutes and strain again.
2. Place a dry skillet over medium heat and stir-fry the shirataki pasta until visibly dry, and makes a squeaky sound when stirred, 1 to 2 minutes. Take off the heat and set aside.
3. For the salmon sauce:
4. Melt half of the butter in a large skillet; season the salmon with salt, black pepper, and cook in the butter until golden brown on all sides and flaky within, 8 minutes. Transfer to a plate and set aside. Add the remaining butter to the skillet to melt and stir in the garlic. Cook until fragrant, 1 minute.

5. Mix in heavy cream, white wine, lemon zest, salt, and pepper. Allow boiling over low heat for 5 minutes. Stir in spinach, allow wilting for 2 minutes and stir in shirataki fettuccine and salmon until well-coated in the sauce. Garnish with the lemon wedges.

Creamy Mussel With Shirataki

Ingredients:

For the angel hair shirataki:

- 2 (8 oz) packs angel hair shirataki

For the creamy mussels:

- 2 tsp red chili flakes

- ½ cup fish stock

- 1 ½ cups heavy cream

- 2 tbsp chopped fresh parsley

- 1 lb mussels, debearded and rinsed

- 1 cup white wine

- 4 tbsp olive oil

- 3 shallots, finely chopped

- 6 garlic cloves, minced

- Salt and black pepper to taste

Directions:

For the angel hair shirataki:

1. Bring 2 cups of water to a boil in a pot over medium heat. Strain shirataki pasta through a colander and rinse very well under hot running water. Remove pot from the heat.
2. Drain and transfer the shirataki into boiling water. Take off the heat, let sit for 3 minutes and strain again. Place a large dry skillet over medium heat and stir-fry the shirataki pasta until visibly dry, 1 to 2 minutes. Take off the heat and set aside.

For the creamy mussels:

3. Pour mussels and white wine into a pot, cover, and cook for 4 minutes. Occasionally stir until the mussels have opened.
4. Strain the mussels and reserve the cooking liquid. Allow cooling, discard any mussels with closed shells, and remove the meat out of ¾

of the mussel shells. Set aside with the remaining mussels in the shells.
5. Heat olive oil in a skillet and sauté shallots, garlic, and chili flakes for 3 minutes. Mix in reduced wine and fish stock.
6. Allow boiling and whisk in the remaining butter and then the heavy cream.
7. Taste the sauce and adjust the taste with salt, pepper, and mix in parsley. Pour in the shirataki pasta, mussels and toss well in the sauce. Serve afterwards.

Roasted Jalapeno Soup

INGREDIENTS:

- ½ cup all-purpose flour
- ¼ tsp salt
- ¼ tsp pepper
- 1 can vegetable broth
- 1 tablespoon olive oil
- 1 tablespoon roasted jalapeno
- ¼ red onion
- 1 cup heavy cream

DIRECTIONS:

1. In a saucepan heat olive oil and sauté onion until tender
2. Add remaining Ingredients: to the saucepan and bring to a boil

3. When all the vegetables are tender transfer to a blender and blend until smooth
4. Pour soup into bowls, garnish with parsley and serve

Cucumber Soup

INGREDIENTS:

- ½ cup all-purpose flour
- ¼ tsp salt
- ¼ tsp pepper
- 1 can vegetable broth
- 1 tablespoon olive oil
- 1 lb. cucumber
- ¼ red onion
- 1 cup heavy cream

DIRECTIONS:

1. In a saucepan heat olive oil and sauté onion until tender
2. Add remaining Ingredients: to the saucepan and bring to a boil

3. When all the vegetables are tender transfer to a blender and blend until smooth
4. Pour soup into bowls, garnish with parsley and serve

Sweetcorn Soup

INGREDIENTS:

- ¼ tsp salt
- ¼ tsp pepper
- 1 can vegetable broth
- 1 tablespoon olive oil
- 1 lb. sweetcorn
- ¼ red onion
- ½ cup all-purpose flour
- 1 cup heavy cream

DIRECTIONS:

1. In a saucepan heat olive oil and sauté onion until tender
2. Add remaining Ingredients: to the saucepan and bring to a boil

3. When all the vegetables are tender transfer to a blender and blend until smooth
4. Pour soup into bowls, garnish with parsley and serve

Baking Powder Bread

Ingredients:

- 3 tablespoons cream cheese
- ½ teaspoon rosemary
- 3 medium eggs
- ¼ teaspoon baking powder
- Salt and pepper to taste

Directions:

1. Start by turning your oven to 350F to preheat it.
2. Use parchment paper to line a baking sheet. Use two bowls to separate the eggs add whites to one dish and the yolks to the other.
3. Add cream cheese to the bowl with egg yolks and use an electric hand mixer to combine everything well.

4. Add baking powder to the bowl with the egg whites. Use an electric hand mixer and combine the Ingredients: until soft peak forms (the eggs should be fluffy).
5. Combine the Ingredients: from the two bowls together. Don't use the mixer here, but just stir everything until you incorporate the Ingredients:.
6. The important thing is to avoid over mixing because it will ruin the volume of the batter. The best way to ensure that the batter is good is to make sure the eggs remain fluffy.
7. Use a spoon to transfer a spoonful of batter at a time to the baking sheet. Your goal is to form flatbread cookie-like form.
8. You should get about 12 servings from the recipe. Bake for 20 minutes at the set temperature.

Cloud Flatbread

Ingredients:

- 3 big eggs
- 1/8 cup cheddar cheese, grated
- 3 tablespoons cream cheese
- 1 tablespoon fresh thyme, chopped

Directions:

1. Start by turning your oven to 350F to preheat it. Use two bowls to separate the eggs put the whites in one bowl and the yolks in the other.
2. Use a whisker to combine the yolks well. Add cream cheese and combine everything well once again.
3. Next, add fresh thyme and cheddar cheese and mix all the Ingredients: well.
4. Use an electric hand mixer to beat the egg whites until stiff peak forms. Add the yolks-

cheese mixture to the whites and make sure to fold it in gently.
5. Use parchment paper to line a baking sheet and grease it with cooking spray.
6. Transfer spoon dollops of the dough into the pan and form the circles of any desired size. Bake for 10 minutes at the set temperature (the top should be golden brown).

Lemon Bread With Blueberries

Ingredients:

- 1 teaspoon tartar cream
- ½ teaspoon vanilla stevia
- ½ teaspoon baking soda
- 1 cup fresh blueberries
- 2 tablespoons whey protein powder
- 1 tablespoon lemon zest
- 3 cups almond flour
- 6 big eggs
- Salt to taste

Directions:

1. Start by turning your oven to 350F to preheat it. Use a food processor or a blender and add almond flour, whey protein powder, baking

soda, tartar cream, and salt to taste to it (you won't need more than ½ teaspoon of salt). Pulse all the Ingredients:.
2. Add lemon zest, eggs, and vanilla stevia and continue pulsing until you get a smooth batter. Add blueberries and stir gently with a spoon or use your hands to incorporate them with the other Ingredients:.
3. Use parchment paper to line a loaf pan and grease it with cooking spray.
4. Bake for 50 minutes at the set temperature. Allow the bread to completely cool down before serving.

Artichoke Spinach Pizza

Ingredients:

- 4 teaspoon dried oregano
- 8 teaspoon black pepper
- (10-ounce) package frozen chopped spinach, thawed and drained
- (1-pound) Italian cheese-flavored pizza crust (such as Boboli)
- (14-ounce) can quartered artichoke hearts, drained
- cup part-skim ricotta cheese
- 4 cup thinly sliced green onions
- 4 teaspoon bottled minced garlic
- 3 cup (2 1/2 ounces) grated sharp provolone or shredded part-skim mozzarella cheese

Directions:

1. Preheat oven to 450°.
2. Combine the first 5 Ingredients: in a medium bowl. Stir in spinach. Place pizza crust on a baking sheet. Spread spinach mixture over pizza crust, leaving a 1/2-inch border; top with artichokes and cheese.
3. Bake at 450° for 13 minutes or until cheese melts.

Arugula Pesto Ricotta And Smoked Mozzarella Pizza

Ingredients:

- 4 teaspoon black pepper
- cup shredded smoked mozzarella
- packed cup (ounce) arugula
- pound pizza dough
- plum tomatoes, sliced 1/4 inch thick
- Cornmeal, for dusting
- 2 cup part-skim ricotta
- garlic cloves, crushed
- 2 teaspoon kosher salt
- tablespoon olive oil

Directions:

1. Preheat oven to 475°. Sprinkle baking sheet with cornmeal.
2. In food processor, blend ricotta, garlic, salt, and pepper until smooth.
3. Add mozzarella and arugula. Pulse to combine.
4. On lightly floured surface, roll pizza dough into a 14-inch circle; transfer to baking sheet.
5. Spread ricotta mixture on top, leaving a 1-inch border. Top with tomatoes and drizzle with oil. Bake 15 to 16 minutes, until the crust is golden.

Bacon And Egg Breakfast Pizza

Ingredients:

- center-cut bacon slices, cooked and crumbled
- cup (4 ounces) reduced-fat shredded extrasharp cheddar cheese
- large egg whites, lightly beaten
- 4 teaspoon salt
- 8 teaspoon freshly ground black pepper
- (8-ounce) can reduced-fat refrigerated crescent dinner roll dough
- Cooking spray
- cup frozen shredded or diced hash brown potatoes, thawed
- tablespoons grated fresh Parmesan cheese

Directions:

1. Preheat oven to 375°.
2. Unroll dough, and separate into triangles. Press triangles together to form a single 10-inch round crust on a 12-inch pizza pan coated with cooking spray. Crimp edges of dough with fingers to form a rim.
3. Top prepared dough with potatoes, bacon, and cheddar cheese. Carefully pour egg whites over cheese; sprinkle with salt, pepper, and Parmesan cheese.
4. Bake at 375° for 23 minutes or until crust is browned. Cut into wedges.

Pitta Pizzas

Ingredients:

- 2 tomatoes, sliced
- 6 slices salami, torn into small pieces
- 50g cheddar, grated
- 4large pitta breads
- 4 tbsp tomato purée
- 2 tsp mixed herb

Directions:

1. Heat the grill. Spread each pitta bread with 1 tbsp tomato purée, sprinkle over the mixed herbs, then lay on the tomato slices.
2. Divide the salami between the pittas, sprinkle over the cheese and grill until the cheese is golden and bubbling.

Pork, Gorgonzola & Garlic Butter Pizza

Ingredients:

- 500g pork mince
- 125g gorgonzola, broken into small chunks
- 1 red onion, finely sliced
- 2 green chillies, sliced
- 50g of rocket
- 20 pitted green olives, sliced
- finely grated zest 1 lemon

For the dough

- 325g strong bread flour
- 1 sachet fast action yeast
- 1 tbsp extra virgin olive oil, plus extra for frying and drizzling

For the garlic butter

- 60g butter, softened

- 2 garlic cloves

- 4 sage leaves, chopped

- 2 tsp tomato purée

Directions:

1. To make the dough, put the flour, yeast and 1 tsp salt into the bowl of an electric mixer with a dough hook.
2. On a medium speed, gradually pour in the oil and 200ml warm water to make a dough.
3. Alternatively, mix by hand and knead on a floured surface. Cover the bowl with cling film and prove for 1 hr or until doubled in size.
4. Meanwhile, fry the mince until browned, then drain on a kitchen towel. Make the garlic butter by beating the butter with the garlic, sage, tomato purée and some black pepper.
5. Heat the oven to 240C/220C fan/gas 8. Divide the dough into four balls. Roll the balls on a

floured surface into thin rounds, about 20cm wide.

6. Lift onto floured baking trays, then spread with the garlic butter, leaving a 1cm border.

7. Sprinkle with the mince, cheese, onion and chilli. Bake for 10-12 mins or until the dough is crisp. Scatter over the rocket, olives and lemon zest, and drizzle over some olive oil to serve.

Gluten-Free Cauliflower Crust Pesto Pizza

Ingredients:

- 1 teaspoon dried oregano
- 1/2 teaspoon salt
- Pinch of crushed black pepper
- 3 tablespoons of your favorite pesto (this swiss chard pesto recipe works well here)
- 1/2 cup grated mozzarella
- 1/2 cup grape tomatoes
- 1 small head cauliflower
- 2 garlic cloves
- 1 egg
- 1/2 cup grated mozzarella
- 1/2 cup grated parmesan

- 1/4 cup fresh basil leaves (for garnish)

Directions:

1. Preheat oven to 425 degrees.
2. Cut cauliflower into florets, remove stems and leaves.
3. Using a food processor, or box grater, grate cauliflower until it resembles rice (make sure not to over process). You should have about 2 1/2 cups of shredded cauliflower. Grate your garlic into the cauliflower "rice."
4. In a medium, non-stick skillet heat cauliflower and garlic for about 5-8 minutes. (This step can also be done in the microwave).
5. Allow cauliflower to cool slightly. Transfer cauliflower "rice" to the center of a clean dish towel. And squeeze out all of the liquid. (This step is essential for making an extra crispy crust!)

6. Transfer dry cauliflower "rice" to a medium-sized bowl. Add the egg, grated mozzarella, grated parmesan, oregano, and salt & pepper.
7. Spread cauliflower mixture onto a parchment-lined baking sheet. Press down to form an 8 inch wide crust.
8. Bake for 12 15 minutes, or until golden brown. Using a rubber spatula, evenly spread pesto on cooked crust. Add grated mozzarella cheese, and grape tomatoes to the pizza. Bake for an additional 5-8 minutes, or until cheese is melted. Garnish with fresh basil leaves.

Pepperoni Pizza Gluten Free, Dairy Free And Egg Free

Ingredients:

For the crust

- 1 tablespoon honey
- 1 tablespoon yeast
- 1 1/2 cup warm water
- 2 tablespoons olive oil
- 3 cups gluten free flour blend*
- 1 teaspoon salt
- 1/4 teaspoon garlic powder
- 1/4 teaspoon baking powder
- 1 tablespoon italian seasoning
- 1 tablespoon sugar

For the toppings

- bottled pizza sauce

- dairy free Daiya cheese

- nitrate free pepperoni

Directions:

1. Preheat oven to 350 degrees.
2. In a small bowl, combine the yeast and 3/4 cup warm water just warm, not hot. Let set for 5 minutes to activate. Add the sugar after two minutes.
3. In a large bowl, combine your gluten free flour blend, salt, garlic powder, baking powder and Italian seasoning. Give it a quick stir with a fork to combine.
4. Using your hands, make a well in the dry Ingredients: and add the yeast mix. Add the olive oil, honey, and the rest of the warmed water (3/4 cups) and stir to combine.
5. Lightly coat a round pizza pan with olive oil. Since we use an airbake pan** with holes, I put my dough on parchment paper first and

flatten it out. I make a dough ball and work from the center to push the dough outwards, making a circle. The crust should be thin.

6. Put the crust in the oven for about 25 minutes, or until it starts to look dry. The crust might crack a little bit, but that's fine, gluten free dough is a little different. It's going to taste awesome, and that's what counts!
7. Take it out of the oven and top it with tomato sauce, dairy free cheese, and nitrate free pepperoni. Put the pizza back in the oven for about 20 minutes until the cheese is all melty and delicious and the edges of the crust are golden.
8. Let it cool for a few minutes.

Gluten Free Pizza Crackers

Ingredients:

- 1/2 tablespoon oregano, dried
- 1/4 teaspoon rosemary, dried
- 1/4 teaspoon garlic powder
- 1 tablespoon olive oil
- 1/4 cup pumpkin, canned
- 1 tablespoon tomato sauce
- 1/4 teaspoon baking soda
- 1/2 cup rice flour, white
- 1/2 cup flour, gluten free
- 1/2 teaspoon sugar
- 1/2 teaspoon sea salt
- 1/2 teaspoon basil, dried

- 1/4 cup Monterey Jack cheese, shredded

Directions:

1. Heat the oven to 350*F.
2. Cut two pieces of parchment paper the size of a baking sheet.
3. In a medium bowl combine all of the Ingredients:, using a spoon.
4. Finish mixing with your hands to form a ball of dough.
5. Place the dough on one piece of parchment paper. Place the other piece of parchment paper on top. Roll the dough between the parchment paper until very thin, about 1/4".
6. Remove the top parchment paper. Cut the dough into squares using a knife or pizza cutter.
7. Sprinkle sea salt on top.
8. Transfer the parchment paper onto a baking sheet.
9. Bake for 25 minutes.

10. Remove from the oven and allow the crackers to cool completely (they will crisp as they cool).
11. Store in a sealed container at room temperature for up to three weeks or in the freezer for long term storage.
12. *You can replace the gluten free flour with all purpose or whole wheat flour. *You can replace 1 Tbsp. of the squash with another pureed vegetable.

Spaghetti Squash Pizza Crust

Ingredients:

- 1/2 cup shredded mozzarella cheese
- 1 tablespoon shredded parmesan cheese
- Kosher salt
- 1 medium/large spaghetti squash
- 1 tablespoon olive oil
- 1 egg, lightly beaten
- Freshly ground black pepper

Directions:

1. Preheat oven to 400°F. Carefully cut your spaghetti squash in half with a large, sharp knife.
2. Remove seeds and stringy guts, and brush the cut sides of the squash with 1 tablespoon of olive oil. Season with Kosher salt and freshly

ground black pepper. Place spaghetti squash, cut side down, on an aluminum-lined baking sheet and roast until tender, about 45-60 minutes.

3. To test if your squash is done, scrap the flesh with a fork. If the strands come off easily, it's done.
4. Let the cooked spaghetti squash cool for about 5 minutes, then scrape all the flesh into a beautiful pile of spaghetti strands. Taste and season with some more Kosher salt and freshly ground black pepper if needed.
5. Measure out approximately 3 and 1/2 cups of spaghetti squash. Reserve rest for another use.
6. Wrap measured-out squash in a cheesecloth, clean kitchen towel, or several layers of paper towels. Squeeze out as much moisture as possible. The drier the squash, the more crispy the crust can get.

7. In a medium mixing bowl, combine the squash, egg, mozzarella cheese, parmesan cheese, and season with Kosher salt and freshly ground black pepper. Press squash in a thin, even layer on a parchment-lined baking sheet and form into an approximate 10-inch circle.
8. Bake at 400°F for approximately 20 minutes. Remove from oven, carefully flip, and cook for another 10 minutes.
9. Add desired toppings and bake until done.

Gluten Free Pizza With A Rice Base

Ingredients:

For the Base:

- 1 tablespoon butter

- 1/2 cup shredded cheese, like mozzarella

- Salt and Pepper to taste

- 3 cups cooked rice (make sure it's gluten free)

- 2 eggs, slightly beaten

For the Toppings:

- 1/4 cup Pizza Sauce (ensure it's gluten free)

- 1 cup Mozzarella Cheese, shredded

Optional Toppings

- 1/4 cup green peppers

- 1/4 red onions, sliced thinly

- 1/4 cup white onions, sliced thinly

- 1 garlic clove, sliced thinly
- Parsley to taste

Directions:

For the Base

1. Heat up your leftover rice, you need 3 cups. In a large bowl mix your rice, eggs, butter, shredded cheese, salt and pepper. Mix well until it comes together into a smooth mixture.
2. Line a cookie sheet with parchment paper.
3. Scoop the mixture into 4 piles on the cookie sheet. Use a spoon (or your hands) to shape the piles into circles of equal size, and width. Make sure you press it together tightly. Smooth the edges.
4. Place in a preheated 450 degree oven and cook for 7 to 8 minutes.

Putting it all together

5. Remove the crusts from the oven. Top them with the sauce.

6. Top with cheese. Top with whatever optional toppings you desire. Place back in the oven for another 5 to 7 minutes. Remove from the oven and place on plates.
7. Serve.

Oat Gluten-Free Pizza Crust

Ingredients:

For the gluten-free pizza crust:

- 170g (~1 3/4 cups) gluten-free oats

- 3 eggs

- 60g cheddar cheese, grated (~3/4 cup grated)

- Salt

- Black pepper

To assemble

- Oil for greasing

- Tomato sauce (or similar)

- Grated cheese

- Your choice of toppings

Directions:

1. Preheat the oven to 190°C (Gas Mark 5 / 375°F).
2. Add the oats to a high-powered blender, and blitz until a fine flour is formed. Transfer the oat flour to a large bowl, and add the eggs, grated cheddar, and some salt and pepper. With clean hands, mix well.
3. Line a baking sheet with baking paper, and lightly grease it.
4. Transfer the pizza dough to the baking sheet, and press it out into your desired shape (mine was a rectangle that measured approximately 11 x 9 inches). You want the crust to be quite thin.
5. When you're happy with your crust shape, place it in the oven for around 15 minutes, until lightly browned.
6. Add the tomato sauce, grated cheese, and your chosen toppings, then return to the oven

for a further 15 minutes, or until the pizza is cooked to your liking.

Beef Alfredo Squash Spaghetti

Ingredients:

For the pasta:

- 2 medium spaghetti squashes, halved
- 2 tbsp olive oil

For the sauce:

- A pinch of nutmeg
- 1/3 cup finely grated Parmesan cheese
- 1/3 cup finely grated mozzarella cheese
- 2 tbsp butter
- 1 lb ground beef
- ½ tsp garlic powder
- Salt and black pepper to taste
- 1 tsp arrowroot starch

- 1 ½ cups heavy cream

Directions:

1. Preheat the oven to 375 F and line a baking dish with foil. Set aside.
2. Season the squash with the olive oil, salt, and black pepper. Place the squash on the baking dish, open side up and roast for 45 to 50 minutes until the squash is tender.
3. When ready, remove the squash from the oven, allow cooling and use two forks to shred the inner part of the noodles. Set aside.
4. Melt the butter in a medium pot, add the beef, garlic powder, salt, and black pepper, cook until brown, 10 minutes.
5. Stir in the arrowroot starch, heavy cream, and nutmeg. Cook until the sauce thickens, 2 to 3 minutes.
6. Spoon the sauce into the squashes and cover with the Parmesan and mozzarella cheeses.

7. Place under the oven's broiler and cook until the cheeses melt and golden brown, 2 to 3 minutes. Remove from the oven and serve warm.

Beef-Asparagus Shirataki Mix

Ingredients:

For the angel hair shirataki:

- 2 (8 oz) packs angel hair shirataki

For the beef-asparagus base:

- 2 large shallots, finely chopped

- 3 garlic cloves, minced

- Salt and black pepper to taste

- 1 lb ground beef

- 3 tbsp olive oil

- 1 lb fresh asparagus, cut into 1-inch pieces

- 1 cup finely grated Parmesan cheese for topping

Directions:

For the angel hair shirataki:

1. Bring 2 cups of water to a boil in a medium pot over medium heat. Strain the shirataki pasta through a colander and rinse very well under hot running water. Drain properly and transfer the shirataki pasta into the boiling water. Cook for 3 minutes and strain again.
2. Place a dry large skillet over medium heat and stir-fry the shirataki pasta until visibly dry, 1 to 2 minutes. Take off the heat and set aside.

For the beef-asparagus base:

3. Heat a large non-stick skillet over medium heat and add the beef. Cook while breaking the lumps that form until brown, 10 minutes. Use a slotted spoon to transfer the beef to a plate and discard the drippings.
4. Heat olive oil in skillet and sauté asparagus until tender, 7 minutes. Stir in shallots and garlic and cook for 2 minutes. Season with salt and pepper.

5. Stir in the beef, shirataki and toss until well combined. Adjust the taste with salt and black pepper as desired.
6. Dish the food onto serving plates and garnish generously with the Parmesan cheese.

Garlic-Butter Steak Bites

Ingredients:

For the shirataki fettuccine:

- 2 (8 oz) packs shirataki fettuccine

For the garlic-butter steak bites:

- Salt and black pepper to taste

- 4 garlic cloves, mined

- 2 tbsp chopped fresh parsley

- 4 tbsp butter

- 1 lb thick-cut New York strip steaks, cut into 1-inch cubes

- 1 cup freshly grated Pecorino Romano cheese

Directions:

For the shirataki fettuccine:

1. Boil 2 cups of water in a medium pot over medium heat.

2. Strain the shirataki pasta through a colander and rinse very well under hot running water.
3. Allow proper draining and pour the shirataki pasta into the boiling water. Cook for 3 minutes and strain again.
4. Place a dry skillet over medium heat and stir-fry the shirataki pasta until visibly dry, and makes a squeaky sound when stirred, 1 to 2 minutes. Take off the heat and set aside.

For the garlic-butter steak bites:

5. Melt the butter in a large skillet, season the steaks with salt, black pepper and cook in the butter until brown, and cooked through, 10 minutes.
6. Stir in the garlic and cook until fragrant, 1 minute.
7. Mix in the parsley and shirataki pasta; toss well and season with salt and black pepper.
8. Dish the food, top with the Pecorino Romano cheese and serve immediately.

Green Pesto Pasta

INGREDIENTS:

- ¼ cup olive oil
- 2 tablespoons parmesan cheese
- ½ tsp black pepper
- 4 oz. spaghetti
- 2 cups basil leaves
- 2 garlic cloves

DIRECTIONS:
1. Bring water to a boil and add pasta
2. In a blend add parmesan cheese, basil leaves, garlic and blend
3. Add olive oil, pepper and blend again
4. Pour pesto onto pasta and serve when ready

Chicken And Broccoli

INGREDIENTS:

- 2 tsp honey
- 1 tsp sesame oil
- 2 cups broccoli florets
- 1 ½ tsp soy sauce
- 1 tsp cornstarch
- Salt
- 1 lb chicken thighs
- 1 ½ tbs sesame seeds
- 2 tsp garlic
- 1/3 cup oyster sauce
- 2 tbs oil
- 1/3 cup chicken broth

- Pepper

DIRECTIONS:

1. Cook the broccoli in hot oil until tender
2. Add the garlic and cook 30 more seconds
3. Place the seasoned chicken in the pan and cook until browned
4. Mix the oyster sauce, honey, soy sauce, chicken broth and sesame oil together
5. Combine the cornstarch with 1 tbs of cold water
6. Pour the oyster mixture over the chicken and broccoli and cook for 30 seconds
7. Add the cornstarch, bring to a boil and cook for a minute
8. Serve topped with sesame seeds

Chicken And Rice

INGREDIENTS:

- 3 tbs olive oil
- 1 ½ cup chicken broth
- 2 lb chicken thigh
- 1 cup rice
- 15 oz salsa
- 3 tsp paprika

DIRECTIONS:

1. Cut the chicken and toss with the paprika
2. Cook in hot oil until browned
3. Add the rice and mix well, cooking 1 more minute to toast the rice
4. Add the broth and salsa and stir
5. Bring to a simmer, then cover and cook for 20 minutes Serve immediately

www.ingramcontent.com/pod-product-compliance
Lightning Source LLC
LaVergne TN
LVHW010217070526
838199LV00062B/4640

9788794477802